The Holy Spirit

The Holy Spirit

NICKY GUMBEL

Alpha

Published by
KINGSWAY COMMUNICATIONS LTD
Lottbridge Drove, Eastbourne BN23 6NT, England.
Email: books@kingsway.co.uk
Printed in the U.S.A.

Contents

Introduction

The three talks that you will find in this little booklet are normally given on the Saturday of the Alpha Weekend. They are grouped together – both on the weekend and here – as each relates to the subject of the Holy Spirit. This teaching on the Holy Spirit is fundamental to a Christian understanding of God.

Many people know a certain amount about God the Father and Jesus the Son, but they haven't heard much about the Holy Spirit, or they find themselves confused about what they have heard! During the three talks we trace the activity of the Holy Spirit from the beginning of time to the present, looking at the impact he has had on people's lives throughout history, and how he can make a difference to our own lives. The talks are designed to be informative but also highly practical, as we discover how each of us can be filled with the Holy Spirit and how he can help us to develop our relationship with God. It has been wonderful to watch the way in which the Holy Spirit has worked in so many people's lives on the Alpha course. I am so grateful to God that despite our failings and weaknesses he remains faithful to us.

Many guests on previous Alpha courses have commented that the weekend away was a very significant part of the Alpha course for them – and we therefore strongly encourage you to go on one if you haven't already. The weekend provides some extended time for you to get to know the others in your Alpha group (or on your Alpha course) a little better, as you relax together away from work and other responsibilities.

If you have any questions about what you read here, may I recommend that you speak to your church leader or another Christian you know and respect? I pray that this little booklet might give you a thirst to experience more of the Holy Spirit's fullness in your life. The Bible assures us that when we thirst and ask, God will give us 'the free gift of the water of life'.

Nicky Gumbel

1

Who Is the Holy Spirit?

I had a group of friends at university, five of whom were called Nicky! We used to meet for lunch most days. When most of us came to faith in Jesus Christ, we immediately became very enthusiastic about our new-found faith. One of the Nickys, however, was slow to get going. He didn't seem excited about his relationship with God, with reading the Bible or with praying.

One day, someone prayed for him to be filled with the Spirit. He was; and it transformed his life. A great big smile came across his face. He became well-known for his radiance – he still is years later. Thereafter, if there was a Bible study or a prayer meeting or a church within reach, Nicky was there. He loved to be with other Christians. He became the most magnetic personality. People were drawn to him and he helped many others to believe and to be filled with the Spirit in the way that he had been.

What was it that made such a difference to Nicky? I think that he would answer that it was the experience of the Holy Spirit. Many people know a certain amount about God the Father and Jesus the Son. But there is a great deal of ignorance about the Holy Spirit. Hence, this book is devoted to the third person of the Trinity.

Some old translations speak of the 'Holy Ghost' and this can make him seem a little frightening. The Holy Spirit is not a ghost but a Person. He has all the characteristics of personhood. He thinks (Acts 15:28), speaks (Acts 1:16), leads (Romans 8:14) and can be grieved (Ephesians 4:30). He is sometimes described as the Spirit of Christ (Romans 8:9) or the Spirit of Jesus (Acts 16:7). He is the way in which Jesus is present with his people. The schoolchild's definition is 'Jesus's other self'.

What is he like? He is sometimes described in the original Greek as the *parakletos* (John 14:16). This is a difficult word to translate. It means 'one called alongside' – a counsellor, a comforter and an encourager. Jesus said the Father will give you 'another' counsellor. The word for 'another' means 'of the same kind'. In other words, the Holy Spirit is just like Jesus.

In this book I want to look at the person of the Holy Spirit: who he is and what we can learn about him as we trace his activity through the Bible from Genesis 1 right through to the Day of Pentecost. Because the Pentecostal movement began at the beginning of the last century it might be tempting to think that the Holy Spirit is a twentieth-century phenomenon. This is, of course, far from the truth.

HE WAS INVOLVED IN CREATION

We see evidence of the activity of the Holy Spirit in the opening verses of the Bible: 'In the beginning God created the heavens and the earth. Now the earth was formless and empty, darkness was over the surface of the deep, and the Spirit of God was hovering over the waters' (Genesis 1:1–2).

We see in the account of the creation how the Spirit of God caused new things to come into being and brought order out of chaos. He is the same Spirit today. He often brings new things into people's lives and into churches. He brings order and peace into chaotic lives, freeing people from harmful habits and addictions and from the confusion and mess of broken relationships.

When God created humankind, he 'formed a man from the dust of the ground and breathed into his nostrils the breath of life, and the man became a living being' (Genesis 2:7). The Hebrew word implied here for breath is *ruach*, which is also the word for 'Spirit'. The *ruach* of God brings physical life to humanity formed from dust. Likewise, he brings spiritual life to people and churches, both of which can be as dry as dust!

Some years ago I was speaking to a clergyman who was telling me that his life and his church had been like that – a bit dusty. One day he and his wife were filled with the Spirit of God, they found a new enthusiasm for the Bible and their lives were transformed. His church became a centre of life. The youth group, started by his son who had also been filled with the Spirit, experienced explosive growth and became one of the largest in the area.

Many are hungry for life and are attracted to people and churches where they see the life of the Spirit of God.

HE CAME UPON PARTICULAR PEOPLE AT PARTICULAR TIMES FOR PARTICULAR TASKS

When the Spirit of God comes upon people something happens. He does not just bring a nice warm feeling! He comes for a purpose and we see examples of this in the Old Testament.

He filled people for artistic work. The Spirit of God filled Bezalel 'with skill, ability and knowledge in all kinds of crafts – to make artistic designs for work in gold, silver and bronze, to cut and set stones, to work in wood, and to engage in all kinds of craftsmanship' (Exodus 31:3–5).

It is possible to be a talented musician, writer or artist without being filled with the Spirit. But when the Spirit of God fills people for these tasks their work often takes on a new dimension. It has a different effect on others. It has a far greater spiritual impact. This can be true even where the natural ability of the musician or artist is not particularly outstanding. Hearts can be touched and lives changed. No doubt something like this happened through Bezalel.

He also filled individuals for the task of leadership. During the time of the Judges, the people of Israel were often overrun by various foreign nations. At one time it was the Midianites. God called Gideon to lead Israel. Gideon was very conscious of his own weakness and asked, 'How can I save Israel? My clan is the weakest in Manasseh, and I am the least in my family' (Judges 6:15). Yet when the Spirit of God came upon Gideon (v. 34), he became one of the remarkable leaders of the Old Testament.

In leadership, God often uses those who feel weak, inadequate and ill-equipped. When they are filled with the Spirit, they become outstanding leaders in the church. A notable example of this was the Revd E. J. H. 'Bash' Nash. As a nineteen-year-old clerk in an insurance office he had come to faith in Christ and was a man who was full of the Spirit of God. It has been written about him that 'there was nothing particularly impressive about him … He was neither athletic nor adventurous. He claimed no academic prowess or artistic talent.'[1] Yet John Stott (whom he led to Christ) said of him: 'Nondescript in outward appearance, his heart was ablaze with Christ.' The obituary in the national and the church press summed up his life like this:

> Bash ... was a quiet, unassuming clergyman who never made the limelight, hit the headlines or wanted preferment, and yet whose influence within the Church of England during the last 50 years was probably greater than almost any of his contemporaries, for there must be hundreds of men today, many in positions of responsibility, who thank God for him for it was through his ministry that they were led to a Christian commitment.
>
> Those who knew him well, and those who worked with him, never expect to see his like again; for rarely can anyone have meant so much to so many as this quietly spoken, modest and deeply spiritual man.[2]

Elsewhere we see the Holy Spirit filling people with strength and power. The story of Samson is well-known. On one occasion, the Philistines tied him up by binding him with ropes. Then, 'The Holy Spirit of the Lord came upon him in power. The ropes on his arms became like charred flax, and the bindings dropped from his hands' (Judges 15:14).

What is true in the Old Testament physically is often true in the New Testament spiritually. It is not that we are physically bound by ropes, but that we are tied down by fears, habits or addictions which take a grip on our lives. We are controlled by bad temper or by patterns of thought such as envy, jealousy or lust. We know that we are bound when we cannot stop something, even when we want to. When the Spirit of God came upon Samson, the ropes became like charred flax and he was free. The Spirit of God is able to set people free today from anything that binds them.

Later on we see how the Spirit of God came upon the prophet Isaiah to enable him 'to preach good news to the poor ... to bind up the broken-hearted, to proclaim freedom for the captives and release for the prisoners' and 'to comfort all who mourn' (Isaiah 61:1–3).

We sometimes feel a sense of helplessness when confronted with the problems of the world. I often felt this before I was a Christian. I knew I had little or nothing to offer those whose lives were in a mess. I still feel like that sometimes. But I know that with the help of the Spirit of God, we do indeed have something to give. The Spirit of God enables us to bring the good news of Jesus Christ to bind up those with broken hearts; to proclaim freedom to those who are in captivity to things in their lives which deep down they hate; to release those who are imprisoned by their own wrong-doing; and to bring the comfort of the Holy Spirit (who is after all the comforter) to those who are sad, grieving or mourning. If we are going to help people in a way which lasts eternally, we cannot do so without the Spirit of God.

HE WAS PROMISED BY THE FATHER

We have seen examples of the work of the Spirit of God in the Old Testament. But his activity was limited to particular people at particular times for particular tasks. As we go through the Old Testament we find that God promises that he is going to do something new. The New Testament calls this 'the promise of the Father'. There is an increasing sense of anticipation. *What was going to happen?*

In the Old Testament God made a covenant with his people. He said that he would be their God and that they would be his people. He required that they should keep his laws. Sadly, the people found that they were unable to keep his commands. The Old Covenant was consistently broken.

God promised that one day he would make a new covenant with his people. This covenant would be different from the first covenant: 'I will put my law in their minds and write it on their hearts' (Jeremiah 31:33). In other words, under the New Covenant the law would be internal rather than external. If you go on a long hike, you start off by carrying your provisions on your back. They weigh you down and slow you up. But when you have eaten them, not only has the weight gone but you also have a new energy coming from inside. What God promised through Jeremiah was a time when the law would no longer be a weight on the outside but would become a source of energy from inside. *How was this going to happen?*

Ezekiel gives us the answer. He was a prophet, and God spoke through him, elaborating on the earlier promise. 'I will give you a new heart and put a new spirit in you,' he said. 'I will remove from you your heart of stone and give you a heart of flesh. And I will put my Spirit in you and move you to follow my decrees and be careful to keep my laws' (Ezekiel 36:26–27).

God was saying through the prophet Ezekiel that this is what will happen when God puts his Spirit within us. This is how he will change our hearts and make them soft ('hearts of flesh') rather than hard ('hearts of stone'). The Spirit of God will move us to follow his decrees and keep his laws.

Jackie Pullinger has spent the last thirty years working in what was the lawless walled city of Kowloon in Hong Kong. She has given her life to working with prostitutes, heroin addicts and gang members. She began a memorable talk by saying, 'God wants us to have soft hearts and hard feet. The trouble with many of us is that we have hard hearts and soft feet.' Christians should have hard feet in that we should be tough rather than morally weak or 'wet'. Jackie is a glowing example of this in her willingness to go without sleep, food and comfort in order to serve others. Yet she also has a soft heart: a heart filled with compassion. The toughness is in her feet, not her heart.

We have seen what 'the promise of the Father' involves and how it is going to happen. The prophet Joel tells us *to whom it is going to happen*. God says through Joel:

> I will pour out my Spirit on all people.
> Your sons and daughters will prophesy,
> your old men will dream dreams,
> your young men will see visions.
> Even on my servants, both men and women,
> I will pour out my Spirit in those days.

(Joel 2:28–29)

Joel is foretelling that the promise will no longer be reserved for particular people at particular times for particular tasks, but it will be for all. God will pour out his Spirit regardless of sex ('sons and daughters ... men and women'); regardless of age ('old men ... young men'); regardless of background, race, colour or rank ('even on my servants'). There will be a new ability to hear God ('prophesy ... dream ...

see visions'). Joel prophesied that the Spirit would be poured out with great generosity on all God's people.

Yet all these promises remained unfulfilled for at least 300 years. The people waited and waited for the 'promise of the Father' to be fulfilled until at the coming of Jesus there was a burst of activity of the Spirit of God.

With the birth of Jesus, the trumpet sounds. Almost everyone connected with the birth of Jesus was filled with the Spirit of God. John the Baptist, who was to prepare the way, was filled with the Spirit even before his birth (Luke 1:15). Mary, his mother, was promised: 'The Holy Spirit will come upon you, and the power of the Most High will overshadow you' (Luke 1:35). When Elizabeth her cousin came into the presence of Jesus, who was still in his mother's womb, she too was 'filled with the Holy Spirit' (v. 41) and even John the Baptist's father Zechariah was 'filled with the Holy Spirit' (v. 67). In almost every case there is an outburst of praise or prophecy.

JOHN THE BAPTIST LINKS HIM WITH JESUS

When John was asked whether he was the Christ he replied: 'I baptise you with water. But one more powerful than I will come, the thongs of whose sandals I am not worthy to untie. He will baptise you with the Holy Spirit and with fire' (Luke 3:16). Baptism with water is very important, but it is not enough. Jesus is the Spirit baptiser. The Greek word means 'to overwhelm', 'to immerse' or 'to plunge'. This is what should happen when we are baptised in the Spirit. We should be completely overwhelmed by, immersed in and plunged into the Spirit of God.

Sometimes this experience is like a hard, dry sponge being dropped into water. There can be a hardness in our lives which stops us absorbing the Spirit of God. It may take a little time for the initial hardness to wear off and for the sponge to be filled. So it is one thing for the sponge to be in the water ('baptised'), but it is another for the water to be in the sponge ('filled'). When the sponge is filled with water, the water literally pours out of it.

Jesus was a man completely filled with the Spirit of God. The Spirit of God descended on him in bodily form at his baptism (Luke 3:22). He returned to the Jordan 'full of the Holy Spirit' and was 'led by the Spirit in the desert' (Luke 4:1). He returned to Galilee 'in the power of the Spirit' (v. 14). In a synagogue in Nazareth he read the lesson from Isaiah 61:1, 'The Spirit of the Lord is on me ...' and said, 'Today this scripture is fulfilled in your hearing' (v. 21).

Jesus predicted his presence

On one occasion Jesus went to a Jewish feast called the Feast of Tabernacles. Thousands of Jews would go to Jerusalem to celebrate the feast, looking back to the time when Moses brought water from a rock. They thanked God for providing water in the past year and prayed that he would do the same in the coming year. They looked forward to a time when water would pour out of the temple (as prophesied by Ezekiel), becoming deeper and deeper and bringing life, fruitfulness and healing wherever it went (Ezekiel 47).

This passage was read at the Feast of Tabernacles and enacted visually. The High Priest would go down to the pool of Siloam and fill a golden pitcher with water. He would then lead the people to the temple where he would pour water through a funnel in the west side of the altar, and into the ground, in anticipation of the great river that would flow from the temple. According to Rabbinic tradition, Jerusalem was the navel of the earth and the temple of Mount Zion was the centre of the navel (its 'belly' or 'innermost being').

On the last day of the feast … Jesus stood up and proclaimed, 'If anyone thirst, let him come to me and drink. He who believes in me, as the scripture has said, "Out of his heart [the original word means 'belly' or 'innermost being'] shall flow rivers of living water" ' (John 7:38, RSV). He was saying that the promises of Ezekiel and others would not be fulfilled in a place, but in a Person. It is out of the innermost being of Jesus that the river of life will flow. Also, in a derivative sense, the streams of living water will flow from every Christian! ('Whoever believes in me', v. 38). From us, Jesus says, this river will flow, bringing life, fruitfulness and healing to others promised by God through Ezekiel.

John went on to explain that Jesus was speaking about the Holy Spirit 'whom those who believed in him were later to receive' (v. 39). He added that 'up to that time the Spirit had not been given' (v. 39). The promise of the Father had still not been fulfilled. Even after the crucifixion and resurrection of Jesus, the Spirit was not poured out. Later, Jesus told his disciples, 'I am going to send you what my Father has promised; but stay in the city until you have been clothed with power from on high' (Luke 24:49).

Just before he ascended to heaven Jesus again promised, 'You will receive power when the Holy Spirit comes on you' (Acts 1:8). But still they had to wait and pray for another ten days. Then at last on the Day of Pentecost: 'Suddenly a sound like the blowing of a violent wind came from heaven and filled the whole house where they were sitting. They saw what seemed to be tongues of fire that separated and came to rest on each of them. All of them were filled with the Holy Spirit and began to speak in other tongues as the Spirit enabled them' (Acts 2:2–4).

It had happened. The promise of the Father had been fulfilled. The crowd was amazed and mystified.

Peter stood up and explained what had occurred. He looked back to the promises of God in the Old Testament and explained how all their hopes and aspirations were now being fulfilled before their eyes. He explained that Jesus had 'received from the Father the promised Holy Spirit' and had 'poured out what you now see and hear' (Acts 2:33).

When the crowd asked what they needed to do, Peter told them to repent and be baptised in the name of Jesus so that they could receive forgiveness. Then he promised that they would receive the gift of the Holy Spirit. For, he said: 'The promise is for you and your children and for *all* who are far off – for all whom the Lord our God will call' (v. 39, italics mine).

We now live in the age of the Spirit. The promise of the Father has been fulfilled. Every single Christian receives the promise of the Father. It is no longer just for particular people, at particular times for particular tasks. It is for *all* Christians, including you and me.

2

What Does the Holy Spirit Do?

Jesus answered, 'I tell you the truth, no-one can enter the kingdom of God without being born of water and the Spirit. Flesh gives birth to flesh, but the Spirit gives birth to spirit. You should not be surprised at my saying, "You must be born again." The wind blows wherever it pleases. You hear its sound, but you cannot tell where it comes from or where it is going. So it is with everyone born of the Spirit' (John 3:5–8).

A few years ago I was in a church in Brighton. One of the Sunday school teachers was telling us about her Sunday school class the previous week. She had been telling the children about Jesus' teaching on being born again in John 3:5–8. She was trying to explain to the children about the difference between physical birth and spiritual birth. In trying to draw them out on the subject she asked, 'Are you born a Christian?' One little boy replied, 'No, Miss. You are born normal!'

The expression 'born again' has become a cliché. It was popularised in America and has been used even to advertise cars. Actually, Jesus was the first person to use the expression of people who were 'born of the Spirit' (John 3:8).

A new baby is born as a result of a man and a woman coming together in sexual intercourse. In the spiritual realm, when the Spirit of God and the spirit of a man or woman come together, a new spiritual being is created. There is a new birth, spiritually. This is what Jesus is speaking about when he says, 'You must be born again.'

Jesus was saying that physical birth is not enough. We need to be born again by the Spirit. This is what happens when we become Christians. Every single Christian is born again. We may not be able to put our finger on the exact moment it occurred, but just as we know whether or not we are alive physically, so we should know that we are alive spiritually.

When we are born physically, we are born into a family. When we are born again spiritually, we are born into a Christian family. Much of the work of the Spirit can be seen in terms of a family. He assures us of our relationship with our Father and helps us to develop that relationship. He produces in us a family likeness. He unites us with our brothers and sisters, giving each member of the family different gifts and abilities. And he enables the family to grow in size.

In this chapter we will look at each of these aspects of his work in us as Christians. Until we become Christians the Spirit's work is primarily to convict us of our sin and our need for Jesus Christ, to convince us of the truth and to enable us to put our faith in him (John 16:7–15).

SONS AND DAUGHTERS OF GOD

The moment we come to Christ we receive complete forgiveness. The barrier between us and God has been removed. Paul says, 'There is now no condemnation for those who are in Christ Jesus' (Romans 8:1). Jesus took all our sins – past, present and future. God takes all our sins and buries them in the depths of the sea (Micah 7:19), and as the Dutch author Corrie Ten Boom used to say, 'He puts up a sign saying "No fishing".'

Not only does he wipe the slate clean, but he also brings us into a relationship with God as sons and daughters. Not all men and women are children of God in this sense, although all of us were created by God. It is only to those who receive Jesus, to those who believe in his name, that he gives the 'right to become children of God' (John 1:12). Sonship in the New Testament (which is used in the generic sense to include sons and daughters) is not a natural status, but a spiritual one. We become sons and daughters of God not by being born, but by being born again by the Spirit.

The Book of Romans has been described as the Himalayas of the New Testament. Chapter 8 is Mount Everest and verses 14–17 could well be described as the peak of Everest.

> Because those who are led by the Spirit of God are children of God. For you did not receive a spirit that makes you a slave again to fear, but you received the Spirit of adoption. And by him we cry, 'Abba, Father.' The Spirit himself testifies with our spirit that we are God's children. Now if we are children, then we are heirs – heirs of God and co-heirs with Christ, if indeed we share in his sufferings in order that we may also share in his glory (Romans 8:14–17).

First of all, there is no higher privilege than to be a child of God. Under Roman law if an adult wanted an heir he could either choose one of his own sons or adopt a son. God has only one begotten Son – Jesus, but he has many adopted sons. There is a fairy story in which a reigning monarch adopts waifs and strays and makes them princes. In Christ, the fairy story has become solid fact. We have been adopted into God's family. There could be no higher honour.

Billy Bray was a drunken and loose-living miner from Cornwall, born in 1794. He was always getting involved in fights and domestic quarrels. At the age of twenty-nine he became a Christian. He went home and told his wife, 'You will never see me drunk again, by the help of the Lord.' She never did. His words, his tones and his looks had magnetic power. He was charged with divine electricity. Crowds of miners would come and hear him preach. Many were converted and there were some remarkable healings. He was always praising God and saying that he had abundant reason to rejoice. He described himself as 'a young prince'. He was the adopted son of God, the King of kings and therefore he was a prince, already possessing royal rights and privileges. His favourite expression was, 'I am the son of a King.'[3]

Once we know our status as adopted sons and daughters of God, we realise that there is no status in the world that even compares with the privilege of being a child of the Creator of the universe.

Secondly, as children we have the closest possible intimacy with God. Paul says that by the Spirit we cry, '*Abba*, Father!' This Aramaic word, *Abba*, is not found in the Old Testament. The use of this word in addressing God was distinctive of Jesus. It is impossible to translate it, but the nearest equivalent translation is probably 'dear Father' or 'Daddy'. The English word 'Daddy' tends to suggest a Western pally relationship to a parent, whereas in Jesus' day the father was an authority figure, and 'Abba', although a term of great intimacy, is not a juvenile word. It was the term Jesus used in addressing God. Jesus allows us to share in that intimate relationship with God when we receive his Spirit. 'For you did not receive a spirit that makes you a slave again to fear, but you received the Spirit of adoption' (v. 15).

Prince Charles has many titles. He is the Heir Apparent to the Crown, his Royal Highness, the Prince of Wales, Duke of Cornwall, Knight of the Garter, Colonel in Chief of the Royal Regiment of Wales, Duke of Rothesay, Knight of the Thistle, Rear Admiral, Great Master of the Order of Bath, Earl of Chester, Earl of Carrick, Baron of Renfrew, Lord of the Isles and Great Steward of Scotland. We would address him as 'Your Royal Highness', but I suspect to William and Harry he is 'Daddy'. When we become children of God we have an intimacy with our heavenly King. John Wesley, who had been very religious before his conversion, said about his conversion, 'I exchanged the faith of a servant for the faith of a son.'

Thirdly, the Spirit gives us the deepest possible experience of God. 'The Spirit himself testifies with our spirit that we are God's children' (v. 16). He wants us to know, deep within, that we are children of God. In the same way that I want my children to know and experience my love for them and my relationship with them, so God wants his children to be assured of that love and of that relationship.

One man who only experienced this quite late in his life is the South African Bishop Bill Burnett, who was at one time Archbishop of Capetown. I heard him say, 'When I became a bishop I believed in theology [the truth about God], but not in God. I was a practical atheist. I sought righteousness by doing good.' One day, after he had been a bishop for fifteen years, he went to speak at a confirmation service on the text in Romans, 'God has poured out his love [that is, his love for us] into our hearts by the Holy Spirit, whom he has given us' (Romans 5:5). After he had preached, he came home, poured himself a strong drink and was reading the paper when he felt the Lord saying, 'Go and pray.' He went into his chapel, knelt down in silence and sensed the Lord saying to him, 'I want your body.' He could not quite understand why (he is tall and thin and says, 'I'm not exactly Mr Universe'). However, he gave every part of himself to the Lord. 'Then,' he said, 'what I preached about happened. I experienced electric shocks of love.' He found himself flat on the floor and heard the Lord saying, 'You are my son.' When he got up, he knew indeed that something had happened. It proved a turning point in his life and ministry. Since then, through his ministry, many others have come to experience sonship through the witness of the Spirit.

Fourthly, Paul tells us that to be a son or daughter of God is the greatest security. For if we are children of God we are also 'heirs of God and co-heirs with Christ' (Romans 8:17). Under Roman law an adopted son would take his father's name and inherit his estate. As children of God we are heirs. The only difference is that we inherit, not on the death of our father, but on our own death. This is why Billy Bray was thrilled to think that 'his heavenly Father had reserved everlasting glory and blessedness' for him. We will enjoy an eternity of love with Jesus.

Paul adds, 'If indeed we share in his sufferings in order that we may also share in his glory' (v. 17). This is not a condition but an observation. Christians identify with Jesus Christ. This may mean some rejection and opposition here and now, but that is nothing compared to our inheritance as children of God.

DEVELOPING THE RELATIONSHIP

Birth is not just the climax of a period of gestation; it is the beginning of a new life and new relationships. Our relationship with our parents grows and deepens over a long period. This happens as we spend time with them; it does not happen overnight.

Our relationship with God, as we have seen in the early chapters, grows and deepens as we spend time with him. The Spirit of God helps us to develop our relationship with God. He brings us into the presence of the Father. 'For through him [Jesus] we both [Jews and Gentiles alike] have access to the Father by one Spirit' (Ephesians 2:18). Through Jesus, by the Spirit, we have access to the presence of God.

Jesus, through his death on the cross, removed the barrier between us and God. That is why we are able to come into God's presence. Often we don't appreciate that when we are praying.

When I was at university I had a room above Barclays Bank in the High Street. We used to have regular lunch parties in this room, and one day we were discussing whether or not the noise we made could be heard in the bank below. In order to find out, we decided to conduct an experiment. A girl called Kay went down into the bank. As it was lunchtime, it was packed with customers. The arrangement was that we would gradually build up the noise. First, one would jump on the floor, then two, three, four and eventually five. Next we would jump off chairs and then off the table. We wanted to see at which point we could be heard downstairs in the bank.

It turned out that the ceiling was rather thinner than we had thought. The first jump could definitely be heard. The second made a loud noise. After about the fifth, which sounded like a thunderstorm, there was total silence in the bank. Everyone had stopped cashing cheques and was looking at the ceiling, wondering what was going on. Kay was right in the middle of the bank and thought, 'What do I do? If I go out it's going to look very odd, but if I stay it is going to get worse!' She stayed. The noise built up and up. Eventually bits of polystyrene started to fall from the ceiling. At that moment, fearing the ceiling would cave in, she rushed up to tell us that we could indeed be heard in the bank!

Since, through Jesus, the barrier has been removed, God hears us when we pray. We have immmediate access to his presence, by the Spirit. We don't need to jump up and down to get his attention!

Not only does the Spirit bring us into the presence of God, he also helps us to pray (Romans 8:26). What matters is not the place in which we pray, the position in which we pray or whether or not we use set forms of prayer; what matters is whether or not we are praying in the Spirit. All prayer should be led by the Spirit. Without his help prayer can easily become lifeless and dull. In the Spirit we are caught up in the Godhead and it becomes the most important activity of our lives.

Another part of developing our relationship with God is understanding what he is saying to us. Again the Spirit of God enables us to do this. Paul says, 'I keep asking that the God of our Lord Jesus Christ, the glorious Father, may give you the Spirit of wisdom and revelation, so that you may know him better. I pray also that the eyes of your heart may be enlightened …' (Ephesians 1:17–18). The Spirit of God is a Spirit of wisdom and revelation. He enlightens our eyes so that, for example, we can understand what God is saying through the Bible.

Before I became a Christian I read and heard the Bible endlessly, but I did not understand it. It meant nothing to me. The reason it did not make sense to me was that I did not have the Spirit of God to interpret it. The Spirit of God is the best interpreter of what God has said.

Ultimately we will never understand Christianity without the Holy Spirit enlightening our eyes. We can see enough to make a step of faith, which is not a blind leap of faith; but real understanding often only follows faith. Anselm of Canterbury said, 'I believe in order that I might understand.'[4] Only when we believe and receive the Holy Spirit can we really understand God's revelation.

The Spirit of God helps us to develop our relationship with God and he enables us to sustain that relationship. People are often worried that they will not be able to keep going in the Christian life. They are right to worry. We can't keep going by ourselves, but God by his Spirit keeps us going. It is the Spirit who brings us into a relationship with God and it is the Spirit who maintains that relationship. We are utterly dependent on him.

THE FAMILY LIKENESS

I always find it fascinating to observe how children can look like both parents at the same time when the parents themselves may look so different. Even husbands and wives sometimes grow to look like each other as they spend time together over the years!

As we spend time in the presence of God, the Spirit of God transforms us. As Paul writes, 'And we, who with unveiled faces all reflect the Lord's glory, are being transformed into his likeness with ever-increasing glory, which comes from the Lord, who is the Spirit' (2 Corinthians 3:18). We are transformed into the moral likeness of Jesus Christ. The fruit of the Spirit is developed in our lives. Paul tells us that 'the fruit of the Spirit is love, joy, peace, patience, kindness, goodness, faithfulness, gentleness and self-control' (Galatians 5:22). These are the characteristics that the Spirit of God develops in our lives. It is not that we become perfect immediately, but over a period of time there should be a change.

The first and most important fruit of the Spirit is love. Love lies at the heart of the Christian faith. The Bible is the story of God's love for us. His desire is that we should respond by loving him and loving our neighbour. The evidence of the work of the Spirit in our lives will be an increasing love for God and an increasing love for others. Without this love everything else counts for nothing.

Second in Paul's list is joy. The journalist, Malcolm Muggeridge, wrote: 'The most characteristic and uplifting of the manifestations of conversion is rapture – an inexpressible joy which suffuses our whole being, making our fears dissolve into nothing, and our expectations all move heavenwards.'[5] This joy is not dependent on our outward circumstances; it comes from the Spirit within. Richard Wurmbrand, who was imprisoned for many years and frequently tortured on account of his faith, wrote of this joy: 'Alone in my cell, cold, hungry and in rags, I danced for joy every night ... sometimes I was so filled with joy that I felt I would burst if I did not give it expression.'[6]

The third fruit listed is peace. Detached from Christ, inner peace is a kind of spiritual marshmallow full of softness and sweetness but without much actual substance. The Greek word and Hebrew equivalent *shalom* means 'wholeness', 'soundness', 'well-being' and 'oneness with God'. There is a longing within every human heart for peace like that. Epictetus, the first-century pagan thinker, said, 'While the Emperor may give peace from war on land and sea, he is unable to give peace from passion, grief and envy. He cannot give peace of heart, for which man yearns more than ever for outward peace.'

It is wonderful to see those whose characters have been transformed into the likeness of Jesus Christ as these and the other fruit of the Spirit have grown in their lives. A woman in her eighties in our congregation said of a former vicar, 'He gets more and more like our Lord.' I cannot think of a higher compliment than that. It is the work of the Spirit of God to make us more and more like Jesus so that we carry the fragrance of the knowledge of him wherever we go (2 Corinthians 2:14).

UNITY IN THE FAMILY

When we come to Christ and become sons and daughters of God we become part of a huge family. God's desire, like that of every normal parent, is that there should be unity in his family. Jesus prayed for unity among his followers (John 17). Paul pleaded with the Ephesian Christians to 'make every effort to keep *the unity of the Spirit* through the bond of peace' (Ephesians 4:3, italics mine).

The same Holy Spirit lives in every Christian wherever they are; whatever the denomination, background, colour or race. The same Spirit is in every child of God and his desire is that we should be united. Indeed, it is a nonsense for the church to be divided because there is '*one* body and *one* Spirit … *one* hope … *one* Lord, *one* faith, *one* baptism; *one* God and Father of *all*, who is over *all* and through *all* and in *all*' (Ephesians 4:4–6, italics mine).

The same Spirit indwells Christians in Russia, China, Africa, America, the UK or wherever. In one sense it is not so important what denomination we are – Roman Catholic or Protestant; Lutheran, Methodist, Baptist, Pentecostal, Anglican or House Church. What is more important is whether or not we have the Spirit of God. If people have the Spirit of God living within them, they are Christians, and our brothers and sisters. It is a tremendous privilege to be part of this huge family; one of the great joys of coming to Christ is to experience this unity. There is a closeness and depth of relationship in the Christian church which I have never found outside of it. We must make every effort to keep the unity of the Spirit at every level: in our small groups, congregations, local church and the worldwide church.

GIFTS FOR ALL THE CHILDREN

Although there is often a family likeness and, hopefully, unity in the family, there is also great variety. No two children are identical – not even 'identical' twins are exactly alike. So it is in the body of Christ. Every Christian is different; each has a different contribution to make, each has a different gift. In the New Testament there are lists of some of the gifts of the Spirit. In 1 Corinthians Paul lists nine gifts:

> Now to each one the manifestation of the Spirit is given for the common good. To one there is given through the Spirit the message of wisdom, to another the message of knowledge by means of the same Spirit, to another faith by the same Spirit, to another gifts of healing by that one Spirit, to another miraculous powers, to another prophecy, to another the distinguishing between spirits, to another speaking in different kinds of tongues, and to still another the interpretation of tongues. All these are the work of one

and the same Spirit, and he gives them to each one, just as he determines (1 Corinthians 12:7–11).

Elsewhere he mentions other gifts: those given to apostles, teachers, helpers, administrators (1 Corinthians 12:28–30), evangelists and pastors (Ephesians 4), gifts of serving, encouraging, giving, leadership, showing mercy (Romans 12:7), hospitality and speaking (1 Peter 4). No doubt these lists were not intended to be exhaustive.

All good gifts are from God, even if some, such as miracles, more obviously demonstrate the unusual acts of God in his world. Spiritual gifts include natural talents which have been transformed by the Holy Spirit. As the German theologian Jurgen Moltmann points out, 'In principle every human potentiality and capacity can become charismatic [ie, a gift of the Spirit] through a person's call, if only they are used in Christ.'

These gifts are given to all Christians. The expression 'to each one' runs like a thread through 1 Corinthians 12. Every Christian is part of the body of Christ. There are many different parts, but one body (v. 12). We are baptised by (or in) one Spirit (v. 13). We are all given the one Spirit to drink (v. 13). There are no first- and second-class Christians. All Christians receive the Spirit. All Christians have spiritual gifts.

There is an urgent need for the gifts to be exercised. One of the major problems in the church at large is that so few are exercising their gifts. The church growth expert Eddie Gibbs once said, 'The level of unemployment in the nation pales into insignificance in comparison with that which prevails in the church.'[7] As a result, a few people are left doing everything and are totally exhausted, while the rest are under-utilised. The church has been likened to a football match, in which thousands of people desperately in need of exercise watch twenty-two people desperately in need of a rest!

The church cannot operate in maximum effectiveness until each person is playing his or her part. As David Watson, the writer and church leader, pointed out, 'In different traditions, the church for years has been either pulpit-centred or altar-centred. In both situations the dominant role has been played by the minister or priest.'[8] The church will only operate with maximum effectiveness when every person is using his or her gifts.

The Spirit of God gives each of us gifts. God does not require us to have many gifts, but he does require us to use what we have and to desire more (1 Corinthians 12:31; 14:1).

THE GROWING FAMILY

It is natural for families to grow. God said to Adam and Eve, 'Be fruitful and multiply.' It should be natural for the family of God to grow. Again, this is the work of the Spirit. Jesus said, 'You will receive power when the Holy Spirit comes on you; and you will be my witnesses in Jerusalem, and in all Judea and Samaria, and to the ends of the earth' (Acts 1:8).

The Spirit of God gives us both a desire and the ability to tell others. The playwright Murray Watts tells the story of a young man who was convinced of the truth of Christianity, but was paralysed with fear at the very thought of having to admit to being 'a Christian'. The idea of telling anyone about his new-found faith, with all the dangers of being dubbed a religious nutcase, appalled him.

For many weeks he tried to banish the thought of religion from his mind, but it was no use. It was as if he heard a whisper in his conscience, repeating over and over again, 'Follow me.'

At last he could stand it no longer and he went to a very old man, who had been a Christian for the best part of a century. He told him of his nightmare, this terrible burden of 'witnessing to the light', and how it stopped him from becoming a Christian. The man sighed and shook his head. 'This is a matter between you and Christ,' he said. 'Why bring all these other people into it?' The young man nodded slowly.

'Go home,' said the old man. 'Go into your bedroom alone. Forget the world. Forget your family, and make it a secret between you and God.'

The young man felt a weight fall from him as the old man spoke. 'You mean, I don't have to tell anyone?'

'No,' said the old man.

'No one at all?'

'Not if you don't want to.' Never had anyone dared to give him this advice before.

'Are you sure?' asked the young man, beginning to tremble with anticipation. 'Can this be right?'

'It is right for you,' said the old man.

So the young man went home, knelt down in prayer and was converted to Christ. Immediately, he ran down the stairs and into the kitchen, where his wife, father and three friends were sitting. 'Do you realise,' he said, breathless with excitement, 'that it's possible to be a Christian without telling anyone?'[9]

When we experience the Spirit of God we want to tell others. As we do, the family grows. The Christian family should never be static. It should be continually growing and drawing in new people, who themselves receive the power of the Holy Spirit and go out and tell others about Jesus.

I have stressed throughout this chapter that every Christian is indwelt by the Holy Spirit. Paul says, 'And if anyone does not have the Spirit of Christ, that person does not belong to Christ' (Romans 8:9). Yet not every Christian is *filled* with the Spirit. Paul writes to the Christians at Ephesus and says, 'Be filled with the Spirit' (Ephesians 5:18). In the next chapter we will look at how we can be filled with the Spirit.

We started the previous chapter with Genesis 1:1–2 (the first verses in the Bible) and I want to end this chapter by looking at Revelation 22:17 (one of the last verses in the Bible). The Spirit of God is active throughout the Bible from Genesis to Revelation.

'The Spirit and the bride say, "Come!" And let those who hear say, "Come!" Let those who are thirsty come; and let all who wish take the free gift of the water of life' (Revelation 22:17).

God wants to fill every one of us with his Spirit. Some people are longing for this. Some are not so sure that they want it – in which case they do not really have a thirst. If you do not have a thirst for more of the Spirit's fullness why not pray for such a thirst? God takes us as we are. When we thirst and ask, God will give us 'the free gift of the water of life'.

3

How Can I Be Filled with the Spirit?

The evangelist J. John once addressed a conference on the subject of preaching. One of the points he made was that so often preachers exhort their hearers to do something, but they never tell them *how* to do it. They say, 'Read your Bible.' He wants to ask, 'Yes, but how?' They say, 'Pray more.' He asks, 'Yes, but how?' They say, 'Tell people about Jesus.' He asks, 'Yes, but how?' In this chapter I want to look at the question of *how* we can be filled with the Spirit.[10]

We have an old gas boiler in our house. The pilot light is on all the time. But the boiler is not always giving out heat and power. Some people have only got the pilot light of the Holy Spirit in their lives, whereas when people are filled with the Holy Spirit, they begin to fire on all cylinders (if you will forgive my mixing metaphors!). When you look at them you can almost see and feel the difference.

The Book of Acts has been described as Volume I of the history of the church. In it we see several examples of people experiencing the Holy Spirit. In an ideal world every Christian would be filled with the Holy Spirit from the moment of conversion. Sometimes it happens like that (both in the New Testament and now), but not always – even in the New Testament. We have already looked at the first occasion of the outpouring of the Holy Spirit at Pentecost in Acts 2. As we go through Acts we will see other examples.

When Peter and John prayed for the Samaritan believers and the Holy Spirit came upon them, Simon the Magician was so impressed that he offered money in order to be able to do the same thing (Acts 8:14–18). Peter warned him that it was a terrible thing to try and buy God's gift for money. But the account shows that something very wonderful must have happened.

In the next chapter (Acts 9) we see one of the most remarkable conversions of all times. When Stephen the first Christian martyr was stoned, Saul approved his death (Acts 8:1) and afterwards began to destroy the church. Going from house to house, he dragged men and women off to prison (v. 3). At the beginning of chapter 9 we find him still 'breathing out murderous threats against the Lord's disciples'.

Within the space of a few days, Saul was preaching in synagogues that 'Jesus is the Son of God' (v. 20). He caused total astonishment, with people asking, 'Isn't he the man who caused havoc in Jerusalem among those who call on this name [of Jesus]?'

What had happened in those few days to change him so completely? First, he had encountered Jesus on the road to Damascus. Secondly, he had been filled with the Spirit (v. 17). That moment, 'something like scales fell from Saul's eyes, and he could see again' (v. 18). It sometimes happens that people who were not Christians, or who were even strongly anti-Christian, have a complete turnabout in their lives when they come to Christ and are filled with the Spirit. They can become powerful advocates of the Christian faith.

At Ephesus, Paul came across a group who 'believed', but who had not even heard of the Holy Spirit. He placed his hands on them, the Holy Spirit came on them and they spoke in tongues and prophesied (Acts 19:1–7). There are people today who are in a similar position. They may have 'believed' for some time or even all their lives. They may have been baptised, confirmed and gone to church from time to time or even regularly. Yet they may know little or nothing about the Holy Spirit.

Another incident occurs early in the Book of Acts and I want to look at it in a little more detail. It is the first occasion when Gentiles were filled with the Spirit. God did something extraordinary which started with a vision given to a man called Cornelius (who had been prepared by the first vision). God also spoke to Peter through a vision and told him he wanted him to go and speak to the Gentiles at the house of this man Cornelius. Halfway through Peter's talk something remarkable happened: 'The Holy Spirit came on all who heard the message. The circumcised believers [ie, the Jews] who had come with Peter were astonished that the gift of the Holy Spirit had been poured out even on the Gentiles. For they heard them speaking in tongues and praising God' (Acts 10:44–46). In the rest of the chapter I want to examine three aspects of what happened.

THEY EXPERIENCED THE POWER OF THE HOLY SPIRIT

Peter had to stop his talk because it was obvious that something was happening. The filling of the Spirit rarely happens imperceptibly, although the experience is different for everyone.

In the description of the Day of Pentecost (Acts 2), Luke uses the language of a heavy tropical rainstorm. It is a picture of the power of the Spirit flooding their beings. There were physical manifestations. They heard a gale (v. 2) which was not a real gale, but it resembled one. It was the mighty invisible power of the ruach of God; the same word as we have seen for wind, breath and spirit in the Old Testament. Sometimes, when people are filled, they shake like a leaf in the wind. Others find themselves breathing deeply as if almost physically breathing in the Spirit.

They also saw something that resembled fire (v. 3). Physical heat sometimes accompanies the filling of the Spirit and people experience it in their hands or some other part of their bodies. One person described a feeling of 'glowing all over'. Another said she experienced 'liquid heat'. Still another described 'burning in my arms when I was not hot'. Fire perhaps symbolises the power, passion and purity which the Spirit of God brings to our lives.

For many, the experience of the Spirit may be an overwhelming experience of the love of God. Paul prays for the Christians at Ephesus that they might have 'power, together with all the saints, to grasp how wide and long and high and deep is the love of Christ' (Ephesians 3:18). The love of Christ is wide enough to reach every person in the world. It reaches across every continent to people of every race, colour, tribe and background. It is long enough to last throughout a lifetime and into eternity. It is deep enough to reach us however far we have fallen. It is high enough to lift us into the heavenly places. We see this love supremely in the cross of Christ. We know Christ's love for us because he was willing to die for us. Paul prayed that we would 'grasp' the extent of this love.

Yet he does not stop there. He goes on to pray that we would '*know* this love that *surpasses knowledge*' – that you would 'be filled to the measure of all the fulness of God' (v. 19). It is not enough to understand his love; we need to experience his love that 'surpasses knowledge'. It is often as people are filled with the Spirit – 'filled to the measure of all the fulness of God' (v. 19) that they experience in their heart this transforming love of Christ.

Thomas Goodwin, one of the Puritans of 300 years ago, illustrated this experience. He pictured a man walking along a road hand in hand with his little boy. The little boy knows that this man is his father, and that his father loves him. But suddenly the father stops, picks up the boy, lifts him into his arms, embraces him, kisses him and hugs him. Then he puts him down again, and they continue walking.

It is a wonderful thing to be walking along holding your father's hand; but it is an incomparably greater thing to have his arms enfolded around you.

'He has embraced us,' says Spurgeon and he pours his love upon us and he 'hugs' us. Martyn Lloyd-Jones quotes these examples among many others in his book on Romans, and comments on the experience of the Spirit:

> Let us realize then the profound character of the experience. This is not light and superficial and ordinary; it is not something of which you can say, 'Don't worry about your feelings.' Worry about your feelings? You will have such a depth of feeling that for a moment you may well imagine that you have never 'felt' anything in your life before. It is the profoundest experience that a man can ever know.[11]

THEY WERE RELEASED IN PRAISE

When these Gentiles were filled with the Spirit they started 'praising God'. Spontaneous praise is the language of people who are excited and thrilled about their experience of God. It should involve our whole personality, including our emotions. I am asked, 'Is it right to express emotions in church? Isn't there a danger of emotionalism?'

The danger for most of us in our relationship with God is not emotionalism, but a lack of emotion – a lack of feeling. Our relationship with God can be rather cold. Every relationship of love involves our emotions. Of course, there must be more than emotions. There must be friendship, communication, understanding and service. But if I never showed any emotion towards my wife, there would be something lacking in my love for her. If we do not experience any emotion in our relationship with God, then our whole personality is not involved. We are called to love, praise and worship God with all of our beings.

It could be argued that emotions are all right in private, but what about the public demonstration of emotion? After a conference at Brighton attended by the former Archbishop of Canterbury there was a correspondence in *The Times* about the place of emotions in church. Under the title 'Carey's charisms' one man wrote:

> Why is it that if a cinema comedy produces laughter, the film is regarded as successful; if a theatre tragedy brings tears to the audience the production is regarded as touching; if a football match thrills the spectators, the game is reviewed as exciting; but if the congregation are moved by the glory of God in worship, the audience are accused of emotionalism?

Of course, there is such a thing as emotionalism, where emotions take precedence over the solid foundation of teaching from the Bible. But as the former Bishop of Coventry Cuthbert Bardsley once said, 'The chief danger of the Anglican church is not delirious emotionalism.' One might add, 'Nor in many other churches.' Our worship of God should involve our whole personality, mind, heart, will and emotions.

THEY RECEIVED A NEW LANGUAGE

As on the Day of Pentecost and with the Ephesian Christians (Acts 19), when the Gentiles were filled with the Spirit they received the gift of tongues. The word for 'tongues' is the same word as that for 'languages' and it means the ability to speak in a language you have never learned. It may be an angelic language (1 Corinthians 13:1) which pre-sumably is not recognisable or it may be a recognis-able human language (as at Pentecost). A young woman called Penny, in our congregation, was pray-ing with another girl. She ran out of words in English and started praying in tongues. The girl smiled and then opened her eyes and started laugh-ing. She said, 'You have just spoken to me in Russian.' The girl, although English, spoke fluent Russian and had a great love for the language. Penny asked, 'What have I been saying?' The girl told her that she had been saying, 'My dear child,' over and over again. Penny does not speak a single word of

Russian. For that young woman those three words were of great significance. She was assured that she was important to God.

The gift of tongues has brought great blessing to many people. It is, as we have seen, one of the gifts of the Spirit. It is not the only gift or even the most important gift. Not all Christians speak in tongues nor is it necessarily a sign of being filled with the Spirit. It is possible to be filled with the Spirit and not speak in tongues. Nevertheless, for many, both in the New Testament and in Christian experience, it accompanies an experience of the Holy Spirit and may be the first experience of the more obviously supernatural activity of the Spirit. Many today are puzzled by the gift. Hence, I have devoted quite a lot of space in this chapter to the subject. In 1 Corinthians 14 Paul deals with a number of questions which are often raised.

What exactly is speaking in tongues?
It is a form of prayer (one of the many different forms of prayer found in the New Testament), according to Paul, 'for those who speak in a tongue do not speak to people but *to God*' (1 Corinthians 14:2, italics mine). It is a form of prayer which builds up the individual Christian (v. 4). Obviously, the gifts which directly edify the church are even more

important, but this does not make tongues unimportant. The benefit of tongues is that it is a form of prayer which transcends the limitation of human language. This seems to be what Paul means when he says 'For if I pray in a tongue, my spirit prays, but my mind is unfruitful' (1 Corinthians 14:14).

Everybody, to a greater or lesser extent, is limited by language. I am told that the average Englishman knows 5,000 English words. Winston Churchill apparently used 50,000 words. But even he was limited to that extent. Often people experience frustration that they cannot express what they really feel, even in a human relationship. They feel things in their spirits, but they do not know how to put them into words. This is often true also in our relationship with God.

This is where the gift of tongues can be a great help. It enables us to express to God what we really feel in our spirits without going through the process of translating it into English. (Hence Paul says, 'My mind is unfruitful.') It is not mindless; it is unfruitful because it is not going through the process of translation into an intelligible language.

In what areas does it help?
There are three areas in which many people have found this gift especially helpful.

First, in the area of *praise and worship*. We are particularly limited in our language. When children (or even adults) write thank-you letters it is not long before they run out of language, and we find that words such as 'lovely', 'wonderful' or 'brilliant' are repeated over and over again. In our praise and worship of God we can often find language limiting.

We long to express our love, worship and praise of God, particularly when we are filled with the Spirit. The gift of tongues enables us to do this without the limitation of human language.

Secondly, it can be a great help when *praying under pressure*. There are times in our lives when it is hard to know exactly how to pray. It can be because we are burdened by many pressures, anxieties or griefs. Not long ago I prayed for a man aged twenty-six whose wife had died of cancer after only one year of married life. He asked for and instantly received the gift of tongues and all the things that he had pushed down in his life seemed to pour out. He told me afterwards what a relief it had been to be able to unburden all those things.

I too have found this in my own experience. In 1987 during a staff meeting at our church, I received a message to say that my mother had had a heart attack and was in hospital. As I dashed up to the main road and caught a taxi to the hospital, I have never been more grateful for the gift of tongues. I desperately wanted to pray, but felt too shocked to form any sentences in English. The gift of tongues enabled me to pray all the way to the hospital and to bring the situation to God in a time of crisis.

Thirdly, many people have found the gift a help in *praying for other people*. It is hard to pray for others – especially if you have not seen them or heard from them for some time. After a while, 'Lord, bless them' might be our most elaborate prayer. It can be a real help to start praying in tongues for them. Often, as we do that, God gives us the words to pray in English.

It is not selfish to want to pray in tongues. Although, 'Those who speak in a tongue edify themselves' (1 Corinthians 14:4), the indirect effects of this can be very great. Jackie Pullinger describes the transformation in her ministry when she began to use the gift:

> By the clock I prayed 15 minutes a day in the language of the Spirit and still felt nothing as I asked the Spirit to help me intercede for those he wanted to reach. After about six weeks of this I began to lead people to Jesus without trying. Gangsters fell to their knees sobbing in the streets, women were healed, heroin addicts were miraculously set free. And I knew it all had nothing to do with me.

It was also the gateway for her to receive other gifts of the Spirit:

> With my friends I began to learn about the other gifts of the Spirit and we experienced a remarkable few years of ministry. Scores of gangsters and well-to-do people, students and churchmen, were converted and all received a new language to pray in private and other gifts to use when meeting together. We opened several homes to house heroin addicts and all were delivered from drugs painlessly because of the power of the Holy Spirit.[12]

Does Paul approve of speaking in tongues?

The context of 1 Corinthians 14 is excessive public use in church of the gift of tongues. Paul says, '*In the church* I would rather speak five intelligible words to instruct others than ten thousand words in a tongue' (v. 19, italics mine). There would be little point in Paul arriving at Corinth and giving his sermon in tongues. They would not be able to understand unless there was someone to interpret. So he lays down guidelines for the public use of tongues (v. 27).

Nevertheless, Paul makes it clear that speaking in tongues should not be forbidden (v. 39). With regard to the private use of this gift (on our own with God), he strongly encourages it. He says, 'I would like every one of you to speak in tongues' (v. 5) and, 'I thank God that I speak in tongues more than all of you' (v. 18). This does not mean that every Christian has to speak in tongues or that we are second-class Christians if we do not speak in tongues. There is no such thing as first- and second-class Christians. Nor does it mean that God loves us any less if we don't yet speak in tongues. Nevertheless, the gift of tongues is a blessing from God.

How do we receive the gift of tongues?

Some say, 'I don't want the gift of tongues.' God will never force you to receive a gift. Tongues is just one of the wonderful gifts of the Spirit, and not the only one by any means, as we saw in the last chapter. Like every gift, it has to be received by faith.

Not every Christian speaks in tongues, but there is no reason why anyone who wants this gift should not receive it. Paul is not saying that speaking in tongues is the be-all and end-all of the Christian life; he is saying that it is a very helpful gift. If you would like to receive it, there is no reason why you should not.

Like all the gifts of God, we have to co-operate with his Spirit. God does not force his gifts on us. When I first became a Christian I read somewhere that the gifts of the Spirit went out in the apostolic age (ie, the first century). They were not for today. When I heard about speaking in tongues I decided to confirm that they were not for today, so I prayed for the gift and then kept my mouth firmly shut! I didn't start praying in tongues and felt that this proved that the gifts had gone out with the apostles.

One day two friends of mine, who had just been filled with the Spirit and received the gift of tongues, came round to see me. I told them quite firmly that the gifts of the Spirit had gone out with the apostolic age, but I could see the difference it had made to them. There was a new radiance about them, and there still is years later. I decided to ask the people who had prayed for them to pray for me to be filled with the Spirit and to receive the gift of tongues. As they did, I experienced the power of the Holy Spirit. They explained to me that if I wanted to receive the gift of tongues, I had to co-operate with the Spirit of God and open my mouth and start to speak to God in any language but English or another known to me. As I did, I received the gift of tongues also.

WHAT ARE THE COMMON HINDRANCES TO BEING FILLED WITH THE SPIRIT?

On one occasion Jesus was speaking to his disciples on the subject of prayer and the Holy Spirit (Luke 11:9–13). In that passage he deals with some of the principal difficulties we may have in receiving from God.

Doubt

There are many doubts people have in this whole area, the principal one being, 'If I ask will I receive?'

Jesus says simply: 'I say to you: Ask and it will be given to you.'

Jesus must have seen that they were a little sceptical because he repeats it in a different way: 'Seek and you will find.'

And again he says a third time: 'Knock and the door will be opened to you.'

He knows human nature so he goes on a fourth time: 'For everyone who asks receives.'

They are not convinced so he says it a fifth time: 'He who seeks finds.'

Again a sixth time: 'To him who knocks, the door will be opened.'

Why does he say it six times? Because he knows what we are like. We find it very difficult to believe that God would give us anything – let alone something as unusual and wonderful as his Holy Spirit and the gifts that come with the Spirit.

Fear

Even if we have cleared the first hurdle of doubt, some of us trip up on the next hurdle of fear. The fear is about what we will receive. Will it be something good?

Jesus uses the analogy of a human father. If a child asks for a fish, no father would give him a snake. If a child asks for an egg, no father would give him a scorpion (Luke 11:11–12). It is unthinkable that we would treat our children like that. Jesus goes on to say that in comparison with God we are evil! If we would not treat our children like that, it is inconceivable that God would treat us like that. He is not going to let us down. If we ask for the Holy Spirit and all the wonderful gifts he brings, that is exactly what we will receive (Luke 11:13).

Inadequacy

Of course it is important that there is no unforgiveness or other sin in our lives, and that we have turned our back on all that we know is wrong. However, even after we have done that, we often have a vague feeling of unworthiness and inadequacy. We cannot believe that God would give us anything. We can believe that he would give gifts to very advanced Christians, but not to us. But Jesus does not say, 'How much more will your Father in heaven give the Holy Spirit to all very advanced Christians.' He says, 'How much more will your Father in heaven give the Holy Spirit to *those who ask him*' (Luke 11:13, italics mine).

If you would like to be filled with the Spirit you might like to find someone who would pray for you.

If you don't have anyone who would be able to pray for you, there is nothing to stop you from praying on your own. Some are filled with the Spirit without receiving the gift of tongues. The two do not necessarily go together. Yet in the New Testament and in experience they often do go together. There is no reason why we should not pray for both.

If you are praying on your own:

1. Ask God to forgive you for anything that could be a barrier to receiving.

2. Turn from any area of your life that you know is wrong.

3. Ask God to fill you with his Spirit. Go on seeking him until you find. Go on knocking until the door opens. Seek God with all your heart.

4. If you would like to receive the gift of tongues, ask. Then open your mouth and start to praise God in any language but English or any other language known to you.

5. Believe that what you receive is from God. Don't let anyone tell you that you made it up. (It is most unlikely that you have.)

6. Persevere. Languages take time to develop. Most of us start with a very limited vocabulary. Gradually it develops. Tongues is like that. It takes time to develop the gift. But don't give up.

7. If you have prayed for any other gift, seek opportunities to use it. Remember that all gifts have to be developed by use.

Being filled with the Spirit is not a one-off experience. Peter was filled with the Spirit three times in the space of chapters 2–4 in the Book of Acts (Acts 2:4; 4:8, 31). When Paul says, 'Be filled with the Spirit' (Ephesians 5:18), he uses the present continuous tense, urging them and us to go on and on being filled with the Spirit.

Notes

1. John Eddison, *A Study in Spiritual Power* (Highland, 1982).
2. *Ibid.*
3. F. W. Bourne, *Billy Bray: The King's Son* (Epworth Press, 1937).
4. J. Hopkins & H. Richardson (eds.), *Anselm of Canterbury, Proslogion Vol I* (SCM Press, 1974).
5. Malcolm Muggeridge, *Conversion* (Collins, 1988).
6. Richard Wurmbrand, *In God's Underground* (Hodder & Stoughton).
7. Eddie Gibbs, *I Believe in Church Growth* (Hodder & Stoughton).
8. David Watson, *One in the Spirit* (Hodder & Stoughton).

9. Murray Watts, *Rolling in the Aisles* (Monarch Publications, 1987).

10. There has been a great deal of discussion in recent years about whether this experience of the Holy Spirit should be described as 'baptism', 'filling', 'releasing', 'empowering' or some other term. For all that has been said and written on the subject, I do not think it is entirely clear from the New Testament which is the right term. What is clear is that we need the experience of the power of the Holy Spirit in our lives. I myself think that the filling of the Holy Spirit is the most faithful to the New Testament and I have used that expression in this chapter.

11. Martyn Lloyd-Jones, *Romans*, Vol. VIII (Banner of Truth, 1974).

12. Wimber & Springer (eds), *Riding the Third Wave* (Marshall Pickering).

Study Guide

by David Stone

The Revd Dr David Stone has devised the following questions to help you get to the heart of what Nicky Gumbel has written and challenge you to apply what you learn to your own life. The questions can be used by individuals or by small groups meeting together.

Who is the Holy Spirit?

1. Do you find the concept of the Holy Spirit frightening (p. 10)?
2. What connection is there between the Holy Spirit and Jesus (p. 10)?
3. What parallels are there between the Holy Spirit's activity in the Bible and today (p. 12)?
4. What main difference is there between what the Holy Spirit does in the Old Testament and what he does in the New Testament – and today (pp. 17f.)?
5. What is the difference between being *'baptised in'* and *'filled with'* the Holy Spirit (p. 21)?
6. What is the result in a person's life when *'rivers of living water'* flow through them (p. 23)?
7. What was Peter's explanation of what happened on the Day of Pentecost (p. 24)?

What Does the Holy Spirit Do?

1. What happens when someone is '*born again*' (p. 28)?

2. What is the primary work of the Holy Spirit in a person *before* he or she becomes a Christian (p. 29)?

3. How does our status before God change *after* we become Christians (pp. 29f.)?

4. How does the Holy Spirit help us '*to develop our relationship with God*' (pp. 35f.)?

5. In what ways does the Holy Spirit make us more like Jesus (pp. 38–40.)?

6. What would you suggest Christians can do to '*keep the unity of the Spirit*' (p. 41)?

7. What does Nicky identify as '*one of the major problems in the church at large*' (p. 44)? Why do you think this is such a problem? What can be done about it?

8. How does the Christian family grow (p. 45)? How is the Holy Spirit involved in this process?

9. Nicky says that although 'every Christian is indwelt by the Holy Spirit ... not every Christian is filled with the Spirit' (pp. 47–48). What advice would you give to someone who wanted to bridge that gap?

How Can I Be Filled with the Spirit?

1. *'In an ideal world every Christian would be filled with the Holy Spirit from the moment of conversion'* (p. 50). Why do you think this doesn't always happen? (p. 51)
2. How important do you think are experiences of the power of the Holy Spirit (pp. 53–55)?
3. Why is the appropriate expression of emotion in our relationship with God so important (pp. 55f.)? How does this differ from emotionalism?
4. What exactly is the gift of tongues for (pp. 57f.)?
5. How would you answer someone who suggested that Christians who don't have the gift of tongues are missing out on something essential (p. 58)?
6. What advice would you give someone who is praying to be filled with the Holy Spirit but had not yet received an answer? (pp. 65–67)

Alpha

This book is an Alpha resource. The Alpha course is a practical introduction to the Christian faith initiated by Holy Trinity Brompton in London, and now being run by thousands of churches throughout the UK as well as overseas.

For more information on Alpha, and details of tapes, videos and training manuals, contact the Alpha office, Holy Trinity Brompton on 0845 644 7544, (home page: www.alphacourse.org), or STL, PO Box 300, Kingstown Broadway, Carlisle, Cumbria CA3 0QS.

Alpha Hotline for telephone orders:
0845 7581 278 (all calls at local rate)

To order from overseas:
Tel +44 1228 611749
Fax +44 1228 514949

Email: alpha@stl.org

Alpha

Alpha titles available

Alpha: Questions of Life   The Alpha course in book form. In fifteen compelling chapters Nicky Gumbel points the way to an authentic Christianity which is exciting and relevant to today's world.

Searching Issues   The seven issues most often raised by participants on the Alpha course: suffering, other religions, sex before marriage, the New Age, homosexuality, science and Christianity, and the Trinity. Also available as booklets.

A Life Worth Living   What happens after Alpha? Based on the book of Philippians, this is an invaluable next step for those who have just completed the Alpha course, and for anyone eager to put their faith on a firm biblical footing.

How to Run the Alpha Course: Telling Others   The theological principles and the practical details of how courses are run. Each alternate chapter consists of a testimony of someone whose life has been changed by God through an Alpha course.

Challenging Lifestyle   Studies in the Sermon on the Mount showing how Jesus' teaching flies in the face of modern lifestyle and presents us with a radical alternative.

The Heart of Revival   Ten Bible studies based on the book of Isaiah, drawing out important truths for today by interpreting some of the teaching of the Old Testament prophet Isaiah. The book seeks to understand what revival might mean and how we can prepare to be part of it.

30 Days   Nicky Gumbel selects thirty passages from the Old and New Testament which can be read over thirty days. It is designed for those on an Alpha course and others who are interested in beginning to explore the Bible.

Why Jesus?   A booklet – given to all participants at the start of the Alpha course. 'The clearest, best illustrated and most challenging short presentation of Jesus that I know.' – Michael Green

All titles are by Nicky Gumbel, who is on the staff of Holy Trinity Brompton